T0051325

For David and Ella, because children's stories
begin with children's questions

This edition published by Kids Can Press in 2019

Originally published under the title *Het hele soepzootje*
by Uitgeverij J.H. Gottmer/H.J.W. Becht bv, Haarlem, the
Netherlands; a division of Gottmer Uitgeversgroep BV

Text © 2018 Floor Bal
Illustrations © 2018 Sebastiaan Van Doninck

English translation © 2019 Kids Can Press

All rights reserved. No part of this publication may be reproduced,
stored in a retrieval system or transmitted, in any form or by any
means, without the prior written permission of Kids Can Press Ltd.
or, in case of photocopying or other reprographic copying, a license
from The Canadian Copyright Licensing Agency (Access Copyright).
For an Access Copyright license, visit www.accesscopyright.ca or
call toll free to 1-800-893-5777.

Published in Canada and the U.S. by Kids Can Press Ltd.
25 Dockside Drive, Toronto, ON M5A 0B5

Kids Can Press is a Corus Entertainment Inc. company

www.kidscanpress.com

The text is set in BioRhyme.

English edition edited by Kathleen Keenan

Printed and bound in Malaysia in 11/2023
by RR Donnelley Asia Printing Solution Limited

CM 19 0 9 8 7 6 5

Library and Archives Canada Cataloguing in Publication

Bal, Floor
[Hele soepzootje. English]
    It started with a big bang : the origin of Earth, you and
everything else / Floor Bal ; Sebastiaan Van Doninck, illustrator.

Translation of: Het hele soepzootje.
ISBN 978-1-5253-0255-8 (hardcover)

    1. Cosmology — Juvenile literature. 2. Universe — Juvenile
literature. 3. Big bang theory — Juvenile literature. 4. Evolution
(Biology) — Juvenile literature. I. Doninck, Sebastiaan Van,
illustrator II. Title. III. Title: Hele soepzootje. English.

QB983.B3513 2019   j523.1   C2018-906328-9

Kids Can Press gratefully acknowledges that the land on which
our office is located is the traditional territory of many nations,
including the Mississaugas of the Credit, the Anishnabeg, the
Chippewa, the Haudenosaunee and the Wendat peoples, and is now
home to many diverse First Nations, Inuit and Métis peoples.

FSC
MIX
Paper | Supporting
responsible forestry
FSC® C144853

It Started with a Big Bang

The Origin of Earth, You and Everything Else

Floor Bal
Sebastiaan Van Doninck

Kids Can Press

This is Earth.

We live on a bright blue ball floating in space.
Our planet is full of humans, animals and plants,
and we all live together in a big tangled web.

It hasn't always looked like that. This is what
the universe looked like a long time ago, long
before we were here. There's nothing.

See? Nothing.

No Earth. No sky, no darkness and no light.

Well, not exactly *nothing* ...

all that nothing, there's one small something — a seed
that will grow into everything else. It's a tiny hot dot
that holds the entire universe inside.

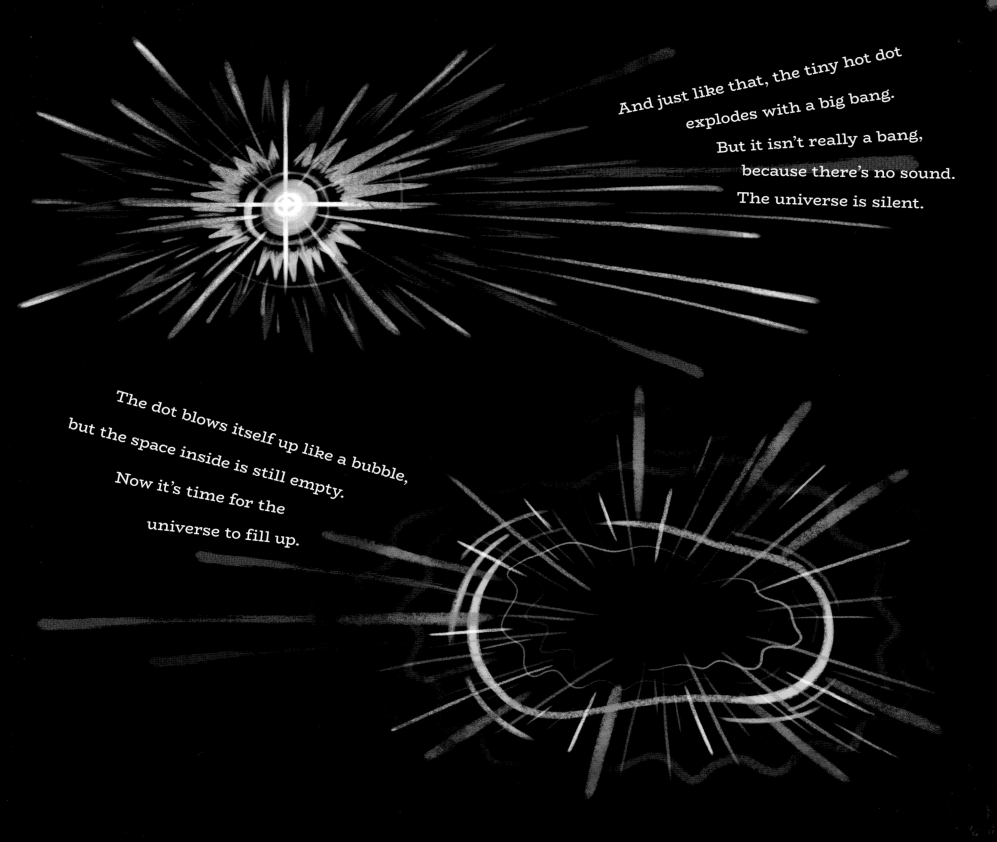

And just like that, the tiny hot dot explodes with a big bang. But it isn't really a bang, because there's no sound. The universe is silent.

The dot blows itself up like a bubble, but the space inside is still empty. Now it's time for the universe to fill up.

Here is the universe.

Look how much is happening!

Stars, moons and suns are spinning all around. Nothing stays the same because everything is moving, all the time.

Sometimes, stars even explode. The explosions leave gas and stardust behind, and pieces of ice and rock, too. They go soaring through space in every direction.

Near the sun, some of the gas, stardust and rock sticks together, forming a ball. The ball grows bigger and bigger, until it is a small planet — planet Earth. Chunks of ice and rock keep raining down. When one of them crashes into Earth, a piece of the ball breaks off.

That small piece of the ball becomes
Earth's moon.

At first, our ball-planet is so hot that water turns into gas. Some of the rock melts, creating a core of molten heat at the center of the ball.

Over millions of years, Earth cools down, and a hard crust of rock forms around the hot core. Slowly, Earth reaches the perfect temperature for water to remain water.

That's how this planet becomes Earth.
The sun is shining and the moon is set in the sky.
It's time for something to grow down below.

This is Earth. It has seas and volcanoes — even underwater volcanoes. The rest of the planet is em...

Water covers most of Earth.
Strong winds blow, and huge waves
crash on rocky islands.
This is no place for something to live.

But **then,** something **does** come to life,
something that likes rough waters. It's almost impossible to see.
It has no head, no eyes and no legs — but it exists.
Then one becomes two, and two become many.

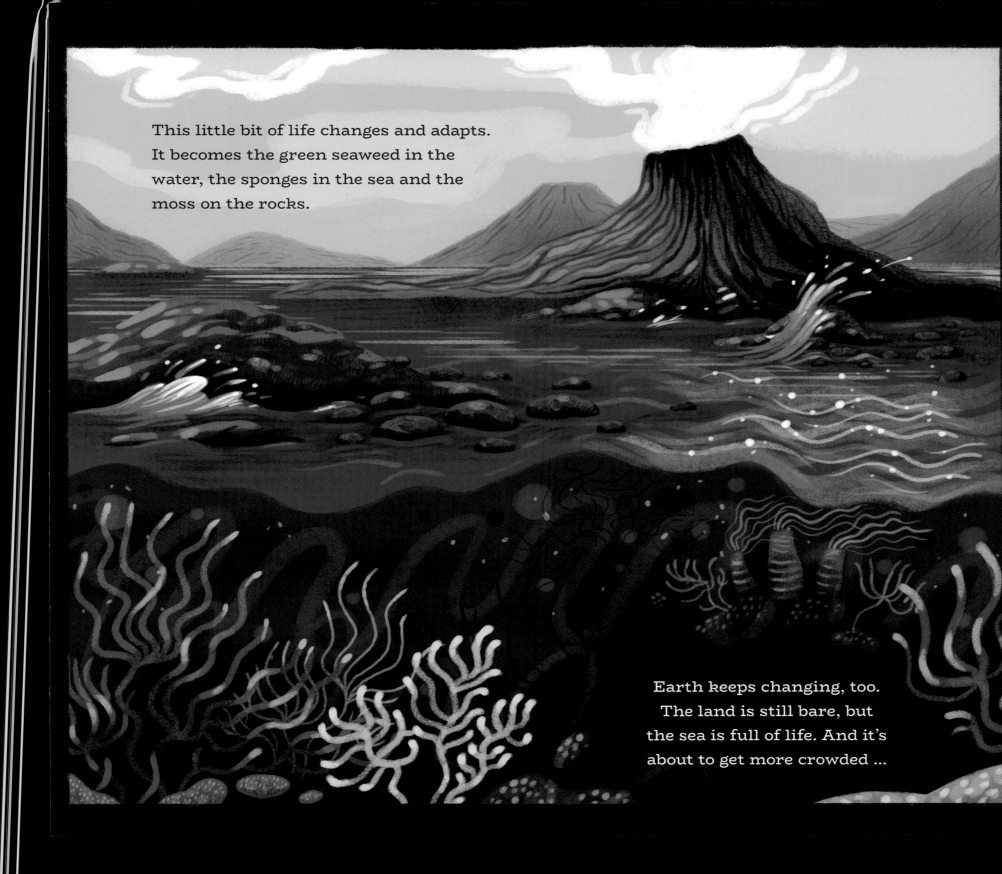

This little bit of life changes and adapts. It becomes the green seaweed in the water, the sponges in the sea and the moss on the rocks.

Earth keeps changing, too. The land is still bare, but the sea is full of life. And it's about to get more crowded ...

This is the ocean, a very big sea.
Many fish and animals live here together.
They all want the same thing:
to eat and not be eaten.

There's plenty of food for the small fish.
And as for the big fish ...
they eat the small fish!

Sometimes one fish has special offspring — babies that can bite extra hard or that have strong fins, almost like legs. Those babies are lucky enough to eat more and escape being eaten.

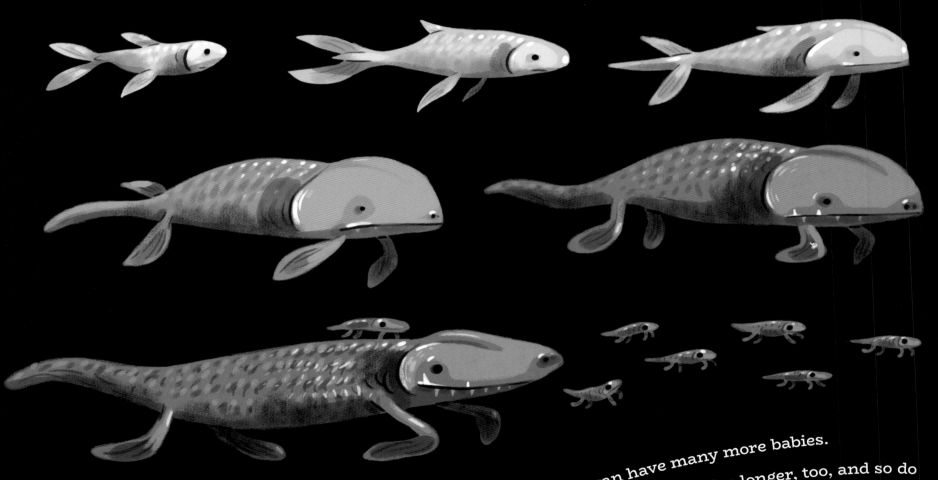

Special offspring live longer, so they can have many more babies. Sometimes those babies have the same luck. They live longer, too, and so do their offspring and their offspring's babies. The entire family adapts, and a new species develops.

Slowly, generation by generation, many of the animals in the ocean change. Some fish even develop real legs.

The ocean is full, but the land is empty. The fish with legs can see land from the water. They're ready to take their first steps.

This is land. Trees and plants grow, and animals
live here, too. Some stay small, but others grow big.
Some become the biggest animals ever: dinosaurs.
A dinosaur's toe is as big as a turtle!

Reptiles and bees fly through the sky.
Starfish share the ocean with giant sharks.

Sometimes it's hot, sometimes it's
freezing cold. In some places it rains,
but in others it's dry. No matter what,
the animals find food. They eat
plants — and one another.

It's a big tangled web.

But suddenly, a giant rock crashes down
from the sky.

BANG!

After the impact, gigantic dust clouds cover
the sun. Everything is dark and cold.

Hardly any plants survive. Only the small animals
can find food to stay alive. Tough break for the
dinosaurs — their time is up.

Now what will live on Earth?

This is Earth, millions of years later. The dust clouds have cleared and the sun shines.

Trees, plants, grass ... the big tangled web is alive and growing. New animals live here, including a kind of ape.

Some of these apes leave the forest to live on wide grassy plains. They spend a lot of time searching for food, so walking on all fours isn't practical anymore. The apes adapt very slowly, but eventually they begin to walk upright on two legs.

They eat plants, and they eat meat, too. They make tools out of stone — knives and axes for hunting. And they make fire to cook the animals they catch.

Eating cooked meat and thinking hard to create tools makes their brains grow bigger, so they get even smarter. Their paws become hands and feet. They lose most of the fur on their bodies.

These apes are smart enough to make plans and solve problems. They can even talk and draw.

Now they've become a new species in the ape family: humans! It's time for something completely different.

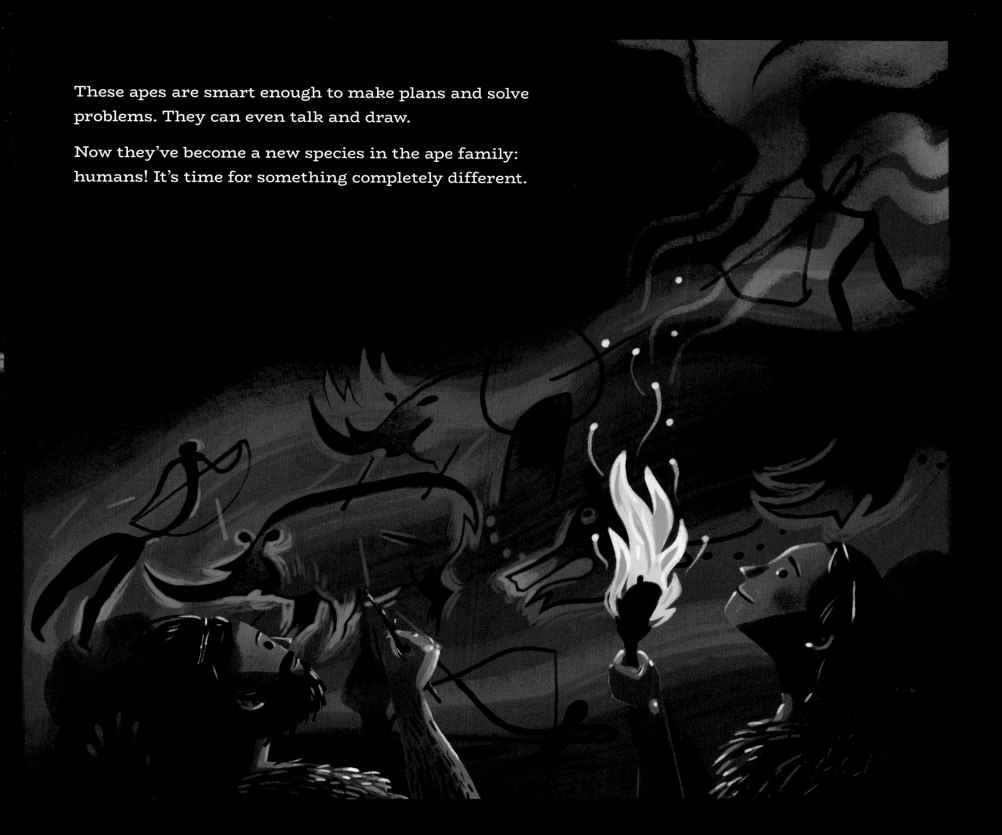

This is the new world humans are building.
They travel all over, searching for places
to live and make a home. They harvest
plants and raise animals.

Humans keep learning. They invent the wheel and the cart so they can travel even farther. They develop a written alphabet, so they can learn to read, write and share what they know with others.

After many years of traveling, inventing and building, humans now live all over. They live close to one another in cities, or far from one another on farms and islands. In all these places, they build. Roads, bridges and homes are everywhere.

Humans can do more than they ever dreamed possible. They dig up dinosaur bones and dive to the bottom of the deepest oceans. They even fly to the moon in rockets and wave to the people back on Earth.

This is Earth, a bright blue ball floating
in space. We live here in a big tangled
web. Humans, animals and plants,
living together ... and it all started with a

big bang.

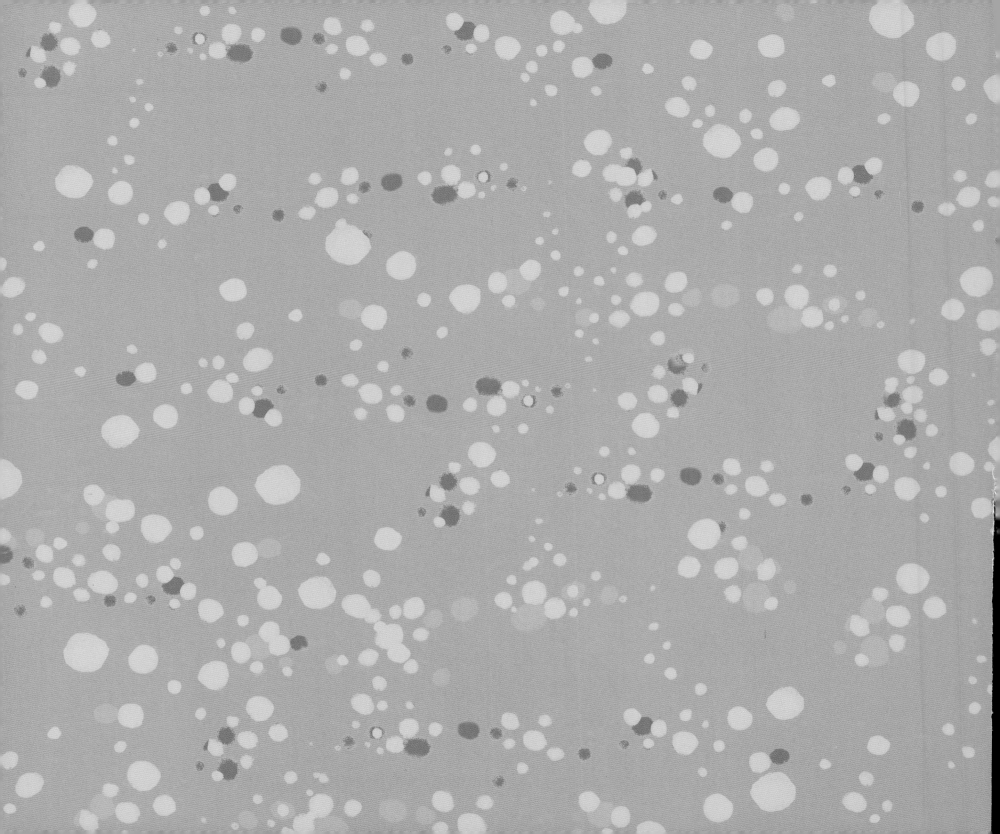